My Leadership Journal
Reflections on becoming a better leader

All rights reserved. Except for use in the case of brief quotations embodied in critical articles and reviews, the reproduction or utilisation of this work in whole or in part in any form by any electronic, digital, mechanical or other means, now known or hereafter invented, including xerography, photocopying, scanning, recording, or any information storage or retrieval system, is forbidden without prior written permission of the author and publisher.

The scanning, uploading, and distribution of this book via the Internet or via any other means without permission of the publisher and author is illegal and punishable by law. Purchase only authorise versions of this book and do not participate in or encourage electronic piracy of copyrighted materials. Your support the author's rights is appreciated.

For ordering, booking, permission or questions contact the author.

Printed in Australia by Blurb.

Introduction

The words journal and journey have the same Latin root, meaning a day. Every leader is on a journey; every day counts as a part of that journey. This leadership journal is intended to engage you in reflecting on your journey at any critical time in your career - whether it's a step up the corporate ladder, a new organisation or leading during a time of major change.

Reflection is not something we do often enough - our days are full, we're busy and there's so much to do that we rely on our existing skills to get us through. However taking time to reflect on our inner lives as leaders is as important as briefly checking the mirror in the morning to make sure our outer image is satisfactory. So why and how would you use a journal for leadership development?

Firstly, the physical act of writing something down promotes learning. It's a combination of making new neurological pathways and ownership ("I wrote it down so it must be true").

And finally, it's practical and there when you need it - at the very times you can't find the time for a leadership course and a 10am thick training folder that you never look at again, your journal sits quietly waiting for you to find 30 minutes a week to learn from your own experience (and learning from experience is where most of our development as leaders comes from anyway).

Here are 4 ways learning journals can be used for leadership development:

1. Part of a formal training program.

Executive programs often promote learning journals - either sent journals out with pre-work material or distributed on the first day of the program. Participants are encouraged to use them to record questions, notes, insights, and action plans.

2. Part of a coaching engagement.

Executive coaches know the value of reflection on personal learning and development. Clients are given a journal as a gift at the beginning of a coaching engagement, and encouraged to write down their goals, actions plans, commitments, what they are learning about themselves, and reflections on assignments.

3. Part of a development assignment.

Stretch assignments and job changes are often used for leadership development. However, what's often missing is taking the time to reflect and debrief with a manager, coach, or mentor.

4. When shadowing.

Shadowing is when you find someone who's really good at something and follow them around to learn how they do it. It's a great way to onboard new managers, or for any manager to get better at something. Journals are used to take notes, jot down questions for follow-up, and for self-reflection.

Whether you're an experienced or an aspiring leader, I encourage you to use a journal as a place of deep personal reflection, a record of your important personal lessons and developments, and a setting for readying yourself to make a difference.

A journal is meant to be a place to record personal reflections, learnings, questions, and notes. It's the property of the learner, and should never be expected to be submitted for review or assessment. Hang on to it - there will be precious content inside to support you in future transitions and challenges.

A guide to leadership journaling

Make time in your schedule once a week to reflect on your leadership performance. You may wish to use the following questions as a guide to your reflections:

• What happened last week that I am particularly proud of? Why am I so proud of that? What impact did it have on my team, other stakeholders, and for the organisation as a whole?

• What happened last week that I'd rather redo if I had the chance? Why do I feel that way? What lessons can I draw from that experience? How would I redo it if I could?

How have I shown up in these areas:

o Communicating my vision and priorities?

o Managing my time?

o Giving people timely feedback?

o Receiving feedback?

o When under stress?

o Authenticity - does my leadership style reflect who I truly am?

Are there any negative recurring patterns in my behaviour?

What aspect of my leadership would I like to improve right now? What could I do this week to support that goal?

Leadership matters. People matter. You matter.
May you always strive to be a more effective leader.

Date:

"Leaders become great, not because of their power, but because of their ability to empower others."

John Maxwell

Date:

"Not the cry, but the flight of a wild duck, leads the flock to fly and follow."

Chinese Proverb

Date:

"Someone's sitting in the shade today because someone planted a tree a long time ago."
                                                                                    Warren Buffett

Date:

"A leader is someone who demonstrates what's possible."
Mark Yarnell

Date:

Date:

"The task of the leader is to get his people from where they are to where they have not been".'

Henry Kissinger

Date:

Date:

Date:

"Do not go where the path may lead, instead go where there is no path and leave a trail."

Ralph Waldo Emerson

Date:

"When you have abandoned all past and future, it is as if you have come alive. You are here, mindful...the nature of all types of consciousness reveals itself."
Ajahn Brahm

Date:

"Great leaders don't blame the tools they are given. They work to sharpen them."
Simon Sinek

Date:

"People don't buy what you do they buy why you do it."

Simon Sinek

Date:

"Leadership is the capacity to translate vision into reality."

Warren G. Bennis

Date: ....

"Try not to become a man of success but a man of value."
Albert Einstein

Date:

"The time is always right to do what's right."

Martin Luther King

Date: ....

"The better you are at surrounding yourself with people of high potential, the greater your chance for success."

John Maxwell

Date:

"Management is doing things right; leadership is doing the right things."
Peter Drucker

Date:

Date:

"Live as if you were to die tomorrow. Learn as if you were to live forever."
Mahatma Gandhi

Date:

"A leader is a dealer in hope."

Napoleon Bonaparte

Date:

"Leadership is about making others better as a result of your presence and making sure that impact lasts in your absence."

Sheryl Sandberg

Date:

"There are three essentials to leadership: humility, clarity and courage."
Fuchan Yüan

Date:

"Great leaders are teachers not tyrants. They help their followers see and understand more. They inspire them to become more and motivate them to do more."

Michael Josephson

Date:

"It is better to lead from behind and to put others in front, especially when you celebrate victory when nice things occur. You take the front line when there is danger. Then people will appreciate your leadership."

Nelson Mandela

Date: ....

"Innovation distinguishes between a leader and a follower."
Steve Jobs

Date:

"We can't solve problems with the same kind of thinking we used when we created them."

Albert Einstein

Date:

"It always seems impossible until it's done."

Nelson Mandela

Date:

"The people who are doing the work are the moving force behind the Macintosh. My job is to create a space for them, to clear out the rest of the organisation and keep it at bay."

Steve Jobs

Date:

"Greatness is not where we stand, but in what direction we are moving."
Oliver Wendell Holmes

Date: ....

"Strategy is about making choices, trade-offs; it's about deliberately choosing to be different."

Michael Porter

Date:

"When a man does not know what harbour he is making for, no wind is the right wind."

Seneca

Date: ....

"Good business leaders create a vision, articulate the vision, passionately own the vision, and relentlessly drive it to completion."

Jack Welch

Date:

"The starting point of all achievement is desire. Keep this constantly in mind. Weak desires bring weak results, just as a small fire makes a small amount of heat."
Napoleon

Date:

"Strategic planning is worthless - unless there is first a strategic vision."
John Naisbitt

Date:

"One important key to success is self-confidence. An important key to self-confidence is… preparation."

Arthur Ashe

Date:

"Efforts and courage are not enough without purpose and direction."
John F. Kennedy

Date: ....

"Transformational leaders don't start by denying the world around them. Instead, they describe a future they'd like to create instead."

Seth Godin

Date:

"Character is the real foundation of all worthwhile success."
John Hays Hammond

Date:

"If we're growing, we're always going to be out of our comfort zone."
John Maxwell

Date: ....

"Nothing great was ever achieved without enthusiasm."
Ralph Waldo Emerson

Date:

"Courage is not the absence of fear. It is going forward with the face of fear."
Abraham Lincoln

Date:

"It is what we make of what we have, not what we are given, that separates one person from another."

Nelson Mandela

Date:

"The roots of effective leadership lie in simple things, one of which is listening. Listening to someone demonstrates respect; it shows that you value their ideas and are willing to hear them."

John Baldoni

Date:

"Nothing in life is to be feared. It is only to be understood."
Marie Curie

Date: ....

"Character is doing the right thing when no-one is watching."

J.C. Watt

Date:

"Dreams are extremely important. You can't do it unless you can imagine it."
George Lucas

Date:

"Life is a great big canvas, and you should throw all the paint on it you can."
Danny Kaye

Date:

"In each of us are places where we have never gone. Only by pressing the limits do you ever find them."

Dr. Joyce Brothers

Date:

"Fortune sides with those who dare."

Date: ....

"No matter how difficult the past, you can always begin again today."
                                                              Jack Kornfield

Date:

"95% of my assets drive out the gate every evening. It's my job to maintain a work environment that keeps those people coming back every morning."

Jim Goodnight, CEO SAS

Date:

"The secret of getting ahead is getting started."
Mark Twain

Date:

"The words you speak become the house you live in."
                                                                Hafiz

Your journey to leadership excellence never ends

Authentic leadership rests heavily on self-concept - this includes the leaders' self-knowledge, clarity of self-image, self-concordance, a merger between the person and the role they hold, and the extent to which the leader's self-concept is expressed in their behaviour.

There is growing evidence that authentic leadership positively impacts follower commitment, engagement and job satisfaction. Promoting cultures of trust, integrity and transparency, authentic leaders are true to themselves, and through leading by example allow others to be the same.

Journaling helps you to develop your life story - those stories that convey about who you are, where you came from and where you are going. These stories give your followers insight into your authenticity, and have been linked to leadership effectiveness.

I hope that you have found journaling an important contributor to becoming a more authentic leader. By chronicling what went well during your leadership interactions or what you could have handled better, you have enhanced your perspective and learned from your actions.

Like all journeys, the completion of one stage typically means time to pause, rest, replenish and plan for the next phase. Your continued commitment to journaling throughout the journey will support your continued ability to self-reflect and learn from your experiences. Seize the opportunity to maximise your development as you prepare for the next stage of your personal leadership journey. Your next journal awaits.

My Influence

My life shall touch a dozen lives
 Before this day is done.
 Leave countless marks of good or ill,
 E'er sets the evening sun.

This, the wish I always wish,
 The prayer I always pray:
 May my life help other lives
 It touches by the way.

Author Unknown

Quick Reference Guide to Journalling Questions

You may wish to use the following questions as a guide to your reflections:

• What happened last week that I am particularly proud of? Why am I so proud of that? What impact did it have on my team, other stakeholders, and for the organisation as a whole?

• What happened last week that I'd rather redo if I had the chance? Why do I feel that way? What lessons can I draw from that experience? How would I redo it if I could?

How have I shown up in these areas:

o Communicating my vision and priorities?

o Managing my time?

o Giving people timely feedback?

o Receiving feedback?

o When under stress?

o Authenticity - does my leadership style reflect who I truly am?

Are there any negative recurring patterns in my behaviour?

What aspect of my leadership would I like to improve right now? What could I do this week to support that goal?

Leadership matters. People matter. You matter.
May you always strive to be a more effective leader.

www.ingramcontent.com/pod-product-compliance
Lightning Source LLC
Chambersburg PA
CBHW060847170526
45158CB00001B/265